Hello!

I am glad you came across this book. Honestly you may know me personally or know someone who knows me personally since I don't expect a lot of people buying and reading it.

But Hey! It's not about the business or scales but doing something interesting and putting my thoughts into writing, which I have been dreaming of doing since a very long time. My close friends always keep telling me that I should rather write my weird and vivid thoughts. So, at last some of my thoughts are here.

Something about the book:

Since I have started to remember and think about things going on around me, I realized that I have a very different way of observing and thinking about society, world and universe. It took me about 15 years to accept the thought that I think very differently as compared to the society around me (except of course a few). I am not saying it is a better way but it is different from general society in this rapidly developing country called India. Rather I sometimes think my way of thinking is rather absurd and worse than others but who knows! I am not sure till now.

So, here it begins, I am on a weekend trip and I had to go out for late night long exposure sky photography but it's raining, so I started space Lo-fi music and I thought maybe it's the right time to write about how I am still trying to understand this world.

I will try my best to make it more understandable and not Abed it (from sit-com show Community) I am not good with grammar and vocabulary so if there's a mistake I might have done that while writing and I fully accept it. Also, if I drift off from reality while writing and things start to make no sense, please throw this book on my face and ask for refund (or you could compliment me too). I'll throw in some random digital arts in the chapter for fun.

Post Edit: I used GPT-4 to find the right title.

Cheers and Enjoy (until you can't).

About the Author:

Author, i.e., me, is an absurdist lazy over thinker who is constantly asking questions about the logics of everyday usual activities and gets fascinated by the facts about how the society, earth and universe have evolved over time.

Author see the world through a very different perspective and find weird ways to deal with situations in daily lives. By profession author is in one of the biggest automotive companies in India working for the design and development of Cars. The author is car enthusiast and tech-geek since childhood. He likes sketching, artwork of cars and other things, driving and travelling to isolated places and mostly reading about technologies, about archeology, biology, paleontology, sociology, bio-chemistry, bio-geology, radiology, psychology, quantum physics, acoustics, astronomy, astrology and many more. The author likes to learn about things and gain knowledge and understanding of the universe.

Author believes that each human and the universe as a whole is a result of complex yet beautiful combination of events and probabilities and we should enjoy the best of it.

Thanks to everyone I met in my life till now for teaching me a lot about this world and I expect to learn more out of it until I live.

I was inspired by all the human beings I have met and known. Rather everyone I could learn from, I learnt and got inspired.

I am especially thankful to a friend of mine who helped me by proof reading this and threatened to leak it if I don't put his name here. To him I would like to say you got played buddy!

Morality!

Since along time Morality was a word which I knew but I could not describe. Sometimes in early teenage years I referred my brother's big fat dictionary to understand what exactly is morality and morals. We didn't have google or internet for that matter in early 2000s.

Now if you search it on internet you will find that morality is basically a system or set of principle to distinct between what is good or bad (right or wrong). It's amusing how I was literally about to write it as "google it".

In the early ages, kids are taught by their parents, family members and teachers (and now internet) about which activities and thoughts are good and which of them are bad. I tried to cram that up but as I started gaining awareness about the word I started wondering why these things are good, bad, right and wrong or for that matter what exactly is good and what exactly is bad.

If you tried asking your Indian parents in childhood then they must have told you that if you keep doing bad things, bad things will happen to you as per karma based principle. I respect it, and so everyone should try to refrain from doing those some bad things.

But, I wondered one night, how would I know if something happened to me, in return of my bad deed(s), is actually bad? May be it is good or may be it's just a matter of perspective. I don't remember exactly but I think I got this thought because a few days prior to this I was studying relative velocity concepts in science class or maybe it was just after the first time I read about Einstein's theory of relativity and it was fascinating.

If that is the case then why are we following the principles of morality? Why even after thousands of years of evolution some things are universally considered bad and others are good. That question haunted me for next 10 years with sleepless nights and brain hurting thinking sessions while blankly staring the walls in my teen years.

Then I started reading and learning about it and somewhere I get the idea that morality principles are somewhat based on survival and progression of human species like if we don't wash ourselves periodically we might die of disease. Some of our ancestors might have died in the age of primordial human beings and so made a pinky swear to ourselves that we will stay clean or not kill any living things unnecessarily and many similar things to keep humanity alive.

I sometimes used to think of it as a selfish act of humanity but then I think if our ancestors wouldn't have followed these principles, when they were really important, then I might not have been here writing about all these things on my digital machine called laptop in a village situated in an isolated valley in Himalayan mountains (pretty selfish thought of mine ha-ha!). But yes it is true that humans are basically selfish and most of (if not all) our decisions are based on our survival.

But, if morality comes down to survival, why humans haven't evolved to beat those odds in their own favorable ways. And things which started to be considered as bad or wrong in early ages because of its potential to affect human survival, still matter enough to humans now. Frankly now I am hoping any intelligent species should evolve in such ways only.

For example, If not cleaning hands is considered bad habit and caused millions of human lives by spreading microbes then why didn't we evolve to have some self-sanitizing sweat or layer on skin. That would be a supercool power but it could have prevented a lot human lives but no we are still washing hands after everything just to keep us alive.

I know recent examples of recorded human evolutions like lactose tolerance in adulthood (basically ability to digest lactose which is present in milk). There are billions of humans right now and we have been on earth (at least modern humans) since thousands of years so why we haven't evolved so that we don't get affected by them. I get a thought sometimes that our ability to solve complex problems using complex tools and phenomenon might be in the way of evolution as we may not need evolution just to stay alive. We can invent now.

I do not promote generally un-acceptable or anti-social acts but I always try to understand how evolution of morality has taken a turn to where we are right now and what would be its future. I expected a little different from an intelligent society which is in existence since thousands of years and is growing rapidly, in terms of setting up the principles of morality from an absolute perspective.

But it may also be possible that humans evolved in such societies following principles of "morality from an absolute perspective" in past and because of its after effects, we lost majority of human lives. Later, it had to be restarted as a new society from old learnings much like Noah's ark or similar to ancient Indian 4 Yuga concept but hey! these are just my thoughts (may not be a reality) and I am still trying to understand how society is working and what is considered to be morally right/good and what wrong/bad and the more I know, the more complex it becomes.

On an add-on thought, what if we get to understand what is good or bad in hypothetical absolute terms. Would we be prosperous forever? I think ideal society is one out of billions of possibilities and probability of us being one is far very less much like any physical constants in modern physics where the value needs to be precise for us to exist if any change have to happen in values of these physical constants, the universe may cease to exist.

I think maybe if we understood the hypothetical absolute morality principles, it might come out be non-existing and our choices in life may be pre-decided as the part of the randomness and entropy. Where the entropy is increasing with time in a random particular way thus deciding the future course including giving us a thoughts that we have free will. But who decides which way this randomness go? May be we decide that much like an observer causes wave function collapse in principle of superposition of particles in quantum physics. It was easily understood with Schrödinger's cat experiment.

Untill we surely prove anything, It is better to believe that society, like universe, works fairly randomly and in a chaotic manner full of diversity and we may have to make peace with it.

Perspective#

Aah! Perspective (that double "a" was really hard to write since my laptops keyboard is not in good condition and that "a" needs a few smacking before it appears on screen).

I wrote in previous chapter how I was so fascinated by the idea of physicality of things being based on observer's perspective, like the Einstein's theory of relativity according to which both space and time are relative and so it is perspective dependent or Quantum mechanics defining that it depends on the observer what the reality is and as observer observes anything it basically causes wave function collapse and thus reality as we observe is formed (fascinating).

I always wonder if the same thing applies to the other physically occurring phenomenon like our thoughts about anything or morality for that matter such that the judgment of good or evil is nothing but a perception. In simpler words what might be good for me may be bad for good for you. I always tested this by thought experiments by mentally placing myself in someone else's position so that I could think If I could have a different perspective of any particular situation of my life (like If I be that person) how would I deal with that.

The results? Every time I thought of a situation from another person's perspective, I always found a very different approach to dealing with the situation or anything for that matter and judgment to the action depends on perspective of observation.

A byproduct of those tests is I always try to understand people's perspective on few things and keep it mapped inside of me so that I could create a meta-image of those people inside my head (its social dilemma kind of thing I guess) for when I have to consider thinking from someone else's perspective I use that memory based meta image. Although now I think it is much more like something meta-identity theft but those identities are safe inside my head. It too has its own disadvantages sadly as it feels much like an out of body experience.

Perspective has a lot of effects if we consider in everyday situation like a stinging bee is flying in my room near the window trying to go out and it is literally bugging me so I might kill it. From my perspective, it is better to do it because it may fall into my food or maybe he will sting me but from his (I am assuming he is a male since he is huge) perspective he is trying hard to understand why normal world is visible but he cannot cross this invisible barrier and he might have lost his family or last chance to procreate but now if I kill him, he may not get a chance of it.

So, is it bad to kill him if he might sting me or affect me? For me it is not, for him it is!

Usually anyone would say kill him before he hurts you, some would say open the window and don't hurt him (but it might have a chance that he will sting me) and a few of the people would immediately leave the room and ask someone for help, may be catch him or kill him so that they don't have to take a fall of hurting an innocent stuck and confused bee. These kind of dilemma comes to my mind every moment and confuse me. Usual people in these situations think of themselves and do every bit to keep oneself safe even though that means killing other intelligent life form.

I got a problem with that because whenever I will go on killing him, he might sting me and it'll be painful to me or I might be able to kill him and it'll be hurtful for him (or probably his family) and there is a slim chance that he might be free to go back to his hive and his family.

If the outcome is painful and lethal to anyone of two of us, we usually think of it as it is nobody's fault because good or bad is just a matter of perspective in this situation (or most of the time in life). As they say in futurama "you got to do what you got to do!"

The opinion we make out of something in our mind is our own perspective. We see the world from our eyes which may be different from the absolute. There can be whole lot of world out there which is away from our perspective. We live in a 3 Dimensional world travelling in time forwards. There might be a path of our existence in 4 dimensional space time which could be represented in a mathematical equation much like every curve in 3 dimensional space. We don't know if there are sentient beings in fourth dimension of time and might just be travelling in 3 dimensional space forward or backward even passing through our bodies because we cannot perceive it.

It all seems sci-fi to everyone but who knows what is out there or here and our brain seems to have hard time understanding it. Consider De-personalization disorder which is basically your brain having out of body experience by making one feel detached from thoughts, feelings and body. So, it gives a very different perspective of your own self. People using LSD have reported having out of body experience also.

Some panic while others cherish the new perspective they get by these experiences depending on how they handle the thought of it. If we cherish those out of body experiences we might just be better human afterwards as it may give self-awareness a whole new meaning.

In ancient Indian lore of Ramayan, the Ravana, in spite of kidnapping sita and many other atrocities, was described as having 10 heads and having super intelligence. I sometimes believed that it may be an artist's impression of his way of thinking or his ability to think from 10 different perspectives. But who knows he might be an evil lord with amputated 10 heads reattached to him. I wonder what would be his metabolism if that were to be true with him being something similar to human.

Scale

The revelation of everything being a relative term seemed like a prime theory but later I realized that perspective is just me thinking a set of things with a set of knowledge in a confined thought zone. Even I don't know how I ended up thinking like that but let me explain. If perspective is a point of observation in 3D space of finite coordinate values (how much area we could observe), then what about if observer goes out of the 3D space? The point of observation would be away in multiple digits of coordinates in 3D space (or may be in 4 D space time)

I remember I was in high school around 2010 - 2011 when we had to cram up the concepts of differentiation and Integration in mathematics. I got no clue what the hell was that back then. But my understanding of the concept evolved as I started studying the same in Physics class and later when I was teaching physics tuitions.

But one fine day I had a fight over some issue with the then girlfriend of mine and I could not sleep, so, I started thinking about the concept of differentiation and integration and its physical ramification (pretty nerdy of me). I was always curious and fascinated with similarities and differences at micro and macro scales while I watched a lot of documentaries about mathematics, quantum physics, space, micro-organisms and many lectures of scientists like Stephen Hawkins and Michio Kaku.

I evolved an Idea that our perspectives on any particular topic might just be equations with different variables for our thought process and these variables may also be specific to each person's perspective and stays limited to one's observation domain. What if the equation is in differential form and if I integrate it to a larger set of range or limits much like definite integral? In simple terms I kick up a notch and think of anything from much larger scale like how my killing of a sting bee would affect the earth revolving around sun which then again is revolving around the Sagittarius A (that's like billion millions X of zoom out may be).

It is a very normal phenomenon in mathematics if we observe a very small segment from a large curvature, it might just seem to be a straight line given the set of variables and least count of observation. So, scale, much like perspective, changes our outcome of observation.

If that is the case then nothing we think or do should matter when observing something from a very large scale as it won't affect something at a very large scale like earth's rotation around sun (It might sound like I am Rick to a Morty). But it affects us or maybe even a local ecosystem at the scale comparable to the observer.

I find it fascinating how similar this sounds to the quantum field theory which paints a picture that every matter has a wave function of quantum field, and in simple terms, every particle is just a ripple in those quantum fields, much like ripple in water and these Quantum fields are spread in space time as omnipresent (like literally everywhere) but our observations of matter or anything in our daily lives is at a very large scale and so we don't see, feel or realize that we may just be in a large ocean of quantum fields and every matter around us may be just ripples in 4 dimensions including we ourselves.

The new revelation expanded the horizons of my thoughts but it also screwed up my thinking pattern in daily life. This thing was too complex since it is not definite which scale to choose and decide what is right or wrong. There was a new variable to my thinking equation as now I have to choose the scale of thought too for decision making or anything.

The same thing applies to humanity and environment at large also I guess. Humans, or for that matter any invasive species too in a local pre-existing ecosystem, cannot avoid but to alter the ecosystem at some scale. Such similar cases have been theorized and proved by geologist and scientist like great event of oxygenation on earth where plant species altered the overall environment of the earth turning it to Oxygen abundant atmosphere.

But if there's an abundance of human processed material from kilometers of depth of oceans to kilometers of heights orbiting around earth and from micro-plastics in living organism's blood to overall increasing the temperature of the whole planet, I mean the scale of impact is much bigger and it tends to affects things which are noticeable at larger scale.

Or we can always have that thought that if we observe from much more larger scale it won't matter. As it has been theorized that we had planet wide changes in past on earth on similar scale because of living organism, I think most likely we are not able to find intelligent life on other planets, in other solar systems and in other galaxies because with the increase in levels of intelligence of a species, there is a higher probability of larger impact on the home planet because of mere existence of it. Think of it this way, to evolve into having such a level of intelligence we had to first secure our survival and expand our population. And so with larger population comes higher probability of causing imbalance in the ecosystem. But it's just my thought and we humans in general don't know the reality as such about it except hypotheses.

In the stinging bee situation, it may not affect the overall hive of bees if I kill one as there might be thousands of them in the area but still if I try to impact their hive then it might be a big mess. But it still won't affect the functioning of the planet as a whole. Planet earth would still be rotating along its axis or revolving around sun in approximately 365 days of time. Or on another note, may be his companion and his team must be searching for him as he might have some important task in the search party of bees.

Thoughts*

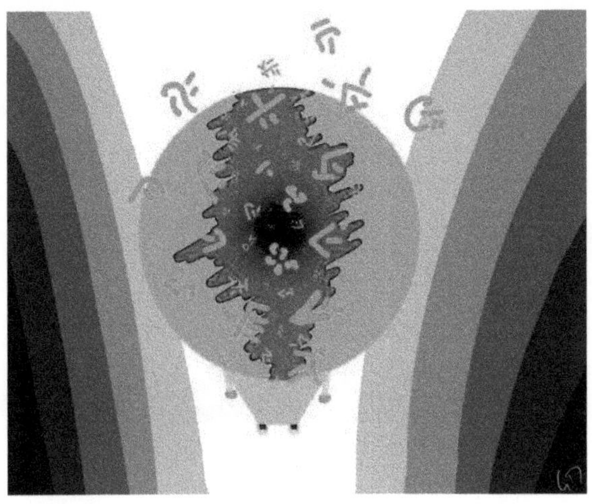

You must be asking yourself, how did I get here? Well I have been writing about how I thought and how my thoughts evolved over time by observing and learning about this world but sometimes one must wonder what exactly a thought is and I always keep thinking about it like a personal thought-inception with layers of thoughts and thoughts existing inside other thoughts.

While driving back from my trip I asked android auto what is a thought? And it referred to Wikipedia which explains it to be a conscious process which can happen independent of any sensory stimulation in most general sense but yes of course there are many theories by great thinkers, scientists and neurologists. I am not going full blow biology or psychology teacher here but I personally developed a few thoughts about thoughts.

From a very limited knowledge of human brains we have, and least of it what I have, I could think of every information inside our brain to be stored in the form of electrical and chemical energy. I am, till this date, really fascinated how we humans have many functions similar to transducers basically converting one form of energy into another form. For example, we get illuminated under sunlight, basically radiations, and convert it to chemical when it produced vitamin D. We inhale oxygen and convert it into chemicals inside our bronchioles and red blood cells which then again are transferred to other cells for further conversion of those chemical compounds to it's by products and utilize the energy for our bodily functions and metabolism.

The same must be going on with the thoughts too, that's what I thought. So, in teenage years I started reading about brain and neurology. I could have tried to become a doctor too but it was a really competitive line of study so I passed. So basics of observation mechanism in our body is when we see something then radiations emitted or reflected by it, in this case light, fall on our eyes and focused on a layer of cells which convert electrical signals according to colors and intensity of it (or may be something more). That electrical signal is converted into chemical and then to electrical in series of neurons in our optic nerve reaching to brain. Where is gets processed by magical process called Cognition. Cognition overall is made out of various cognitive functions like interpreting the chemical and electrical inputs from organs like eye and various other senses including other parts of brain too, processing those signals under a set of rules and then taking actions against it. It seems magical to me since we humans have a hard time explaining how so many cognitive functions happen in our brain.

But gist here is that many things are stored in brain in electrical and chemical form. Then comes Pre-frontal cortex, the famous part of brain considered responsible for important things like planning, decision making, working memory, personality, social behaviors and certain aspects of language besides controlling our thoughts. It does so by having so many neural connections with other parts of the brain and most likely by taking inputs from them.

In previous chapters I wrote about how I always thought that thoughts might just be (or can be represented) as functions of equations with different self-learning and developing variables much like how we are trying to design the

Artificial intelligence. In non-nerd language when we know the feeling of hot we learn that we should stay away from hot objects. So, if these are some self-developing variables then there might be some constants in these thought equations too which we inherited from our parental lineage like keeping our-self safe and functioning and so we refrain from putting our self in dangerous situations generally. Except when one wants to get hormonal high or one is in a state of cognitive impairment. In earlier chapters when I commented that humans might be selfish I think it is important for our survival and I think constants like these in thought equations might has been transferred from our previous generations to us. These might have been variables back then but after due learning it is now constant that we got to keep ourselves alive.

So what I am trying to express here is that our thought equations are dependent on what inputs we get from our senses, what we inherit from our parents and how we process it. In short form, there is a probability that we can define a person's thought pattern in a form of mathematical equations (I am hoping someone might be working on that). It all seems like a fantasy like I saw a sci-fi video of a song (Anvil by Lorn from album Vessel) where human body dies but their thoughts or soul kind of things are stored in electrical storage devices. It might just be a way to achieve immortality in distant future (who knows?).

I also wonder there is also a very strong variable of entropy or randomness of the universe as a system around our thought equations. I wish someone could prove it with experiment like if we make a clone out of our-self with same memory same thought process, a pure physical replica, and record opinions of both of us on any topic. If entropy or randomness of universe is to play a role in it, both of the original and close will have different opinions and will choose differently for any actions. The only variable in this situation would be that those are two different persons and so something else might also play a key role in making us think what we are thinking. If they get same opinion then I may be wrong but it'll be so cool to study that.

I read a few studies where thought tracking was being done and sometimes thoughts to act or response in brain emerged even before there was any stimulus or input. Basically sometimes our pre-frontal cortex is predicting future out of nowhere and that is the reason may be we sometimes say things before thinking. It's like our thought center doesn't even need inputs sometimes to understand the environment and reality as such and gives a response which seems so much fascinating. If there is an ability such like this, I wonder if the reality, as we perceive it to be, might just be fabricated only by the thoughts in our brain and how we perceive it may be regulated by one of the many cognitive functions in our brain. Humans have known similar manipulative cognitive functions in our brain like adjustment of vision as per the blind spot in our vision.

Certainly thoughts are mysterious and there are unknown variables to those thought equations in our brain making it much more complex similar to the DNA profiles. I wonder if we could develop CRISPR kind of method to alter the thought equations too. But then it will be inhuman and used for personal benefits.

I know my pre-frontal cortex have very weird thought equations and I alter big parts of those variables to think of anything from a different perspective sometimes. I casually tell some of my friends that I might be an alien who is here to observe humans. It seems that way to me at-least when I see regular human activities in action and try to think about it from multiple perspectives. I sometimes change my thought equation so much that usual thoughts of human lives sometimes seem very different and so my thought equation seems alien.

Next time you think anything, remember how your way of thinking is always in a definite pattern and slowly develops throughout as you experience variability of life in form of external stimulus.

The thought of killing the sting bee might have been because of the constant in my equation shouting in brain's internal language that it is dangerous. It'll be sending all the SOS signals to prefrontal cortex that learn from me I know from my ancestral knowledge that a bee with a sting is no go zone. And I think the weightage or the degree of those constants in the equations must be really high. I guess these constants are embedded in our DNA profile too otherwise how would be get it inherited in us.

Religion@

Before you think of anything, I am not a religious fundamentalist or radicalist. But I like to think about how religions affects our lives and how I think it might have evolved. I hope I don't offend anyone because of their faith and beliefs.

Religion is something which was really simple yet tough to understand for me. My family is religious and so many of the thoughts I got to learn from them were unexplainable to my brain. When I was younger I did followed but then adulthood hit me and I started thinking of explaining religious practices to myself through scientific principles I know or I think may be present.

I tried seeing it from many different perspectives like how general religious practices from every religion affects our social lives, our brain chemistry and our general physical and mental health and in all those perspectives, conclusion came out to be that religions have a very important role in society and when they were started in history or since when they have existed in human history, they were more closely based on general human rules and duties for the betterment of society at those times and beyond. But I think now religions are slightly misinterpreted and radicalism exist in society.

Humans are in large numbers and have a general tendency to explore and achieve something new. Humans are curious beings and so there's a possibility of humans having compulsive thoughts about things in life which may be considered anti-social or anti human. Or may be a portion of humans have relativity less developed pre-frontal cortex or areas of brain capable of thinking things through, evaluating the situations and deep layered thoughts with less complex thought equations. It might be difficult for them to follow certain rules and so it must have been necessary in some religions to make a concept of punishment or repenting certain "wrong" doings.

Also, for some cases it might be difficult to answer some really basic yet complex answers like what is life and what is our purpose? Why do we live? And a concept of higher power and general sense of being looked by someone having a bigger and better agenda controlling our lives may well be a point of relief for a larger human kind. Or it might just be true that we are being looked and controlled by a higher power. It's a belief thing were if the concept is embedded into your brain, it's probably for the best that you believe and follow it for your own peace of mind.

It's fascinating how thought of existence of a stronger, better entities who are in control of every situation can alter our brain chemistry to make us more sane and at peace with the randomness of the world. It is like our brain choses to believe in it because it is not able to find any other explanation to otherwise unexplainable phenomenon or events. It is fairly reasonable to do so for majority of human population while others toil around the ideas of atheism and science to explain those phenomenon.

I personally believe most of the miracles we find in old stories and literatures of various religions can be explained with concept of science but proving them is a whole together different story. We have come across a lot in the modern history of human existence and science have helped explain a lot. I always get one example of people being possessed by spirits and doing weird behavior which most of scientists now think of it as effects of some neurological disorders or pathogens. Let's take an example of rabies, where if you are not treated timely the symptoms may make you look like a zombie with cerebral dysfunction causing anxiety, hallucinations, hydrophobia, aerophobia and excessive salivation. It seems fairly similar to being possessed to me. Healing them in old ages might have some scientific explanations or may be even placebo.

Even the concept of God is something which I have always struggled to understand. As much as I know about ancient Hindu religion, essentially at the core, there is existence of god in everything and it was a regular practice to thank every resource important for human society including water, air, ground/soil, fire, trees, flowers, animals, birds, sun and even moon to mention a few. The concept was clear as to respect everything that is keeping us alive and functioning and not degrade them. While Christian religion was fairly new, the concept was similar here too for those who seek relief from the thought of randomness in the universe and kind of feel lost with no guidance, there is a presence of god, principles to follow for a better society and concept of repercussions if fail to do so. Even if you read the early developments of Muslim religion or for that matter any other religion, there are similar concepts.

All of the religions have at the core that human species should survive and perish free of diseases, enhance knowledge and wisdom of its own and stay in harmony with any intelligent life form as per the times we live in and if anything guides you or inspires you to threaten human species and its existence then is it is not religious act.

In some ways, religious rules were, and in some cases till now are, basically laws and duties of better human beings. In contrast to modern day laws and regulations these were in form of preaching and it shows a lot about modern society to me sometimes. While on the other hand modern day religions have become much more complex and deviated from the primary reasons of their origination.

In my opinion, religions should adapt and change with times with core values being the same and not the complex multi-national organizations. The religion should be as simple as do well for humans and it'll be good for the society. I mean at the core we all are humans and have same core values and have similar thought equations in our brains.

In modern science, the concept of god is considered somewhat fictional even though many of scientists were and are not atheist. It would be so cool if we eventually find the god entity with modern science. In recent years, the closest modern science has come to the god is Higgs-boson particle which is really the god particle giving mass to every fundamental particle. We humans have discovered its presence but know very little about it till now. The concept of Higgs field and it's mechanism to give mass to any fundamental particle is so out of or pre-conception of existence of matter that it is considered the closest to god entity and so is being referred as god particle. They give mass to any particular fundamental mass less particle and if not done, there won't be any matter around us, just a pool of fundamental mass less particles popping in and out of the existence as they travel at speeds of light. So, no galaxies, no elements and compounds, no sun, no water or earth, no human, animals or plants for that matter would have existed if there wasn't any Higgs field around. Some say it might be true god but we don't know why it happens or who controls the mechanism of Higgs field.

There are new thoughts of agnosticism too in our society. The concept is neither in denial or presence of god but the reality that finding out the absolute existence of god is highly unlikely if not impossible for human beings. It is beyond the scope of human comprehension to learn the true god as per the concept of agnosticism which seems to be true considering how the increase in knowledge of humans is slow comparison to the possibility of our mere existence coming to the end with changes in our local ecosystem.

I guess we would not be sure anytime soon as to how principles of religion which originated in early human ages had a concept of god so complex and yet relatable to the nature of existence of matter. Or may be its similar to pareidolia in our brain which connects the two concepts of god. The one who created the matter and universe as we know it and the one who we worship in different religions.

Mortality&

I tried to write all the previous chapters in a few days just to keep the train of thoughts pure and uninterrupted and so I didn't get a chance to think through anything and it was all impromptu but it took me a dedicated time to think about this chapter. When I first decided that the last chapter would be mortality, I thought of it as end of thoughts, end of the book and end of my writing which I might be doing for the last time. But I am not sure, Its Schrödinger's cat situation.

Whenever we talk about mortality somehow people sound serious and most often religious. It's like mortality has a particular importance in all the religion. Some say our consciousness either goes to swarg lok, heaven, Jannat (a good place) or nark lok, hell, Jahannum (a place for punishment). Some believe in rebirth and coming back in another life form. So mortality is nothing but a phase change if somehow our consciousness lives in another good or bad place or may be here as someone else in different times. The idea of us being mortal makes many people fear most probably because of the introspective thought of losing someone because of death. If I think it from the theory of karma and rebirth, mortality is just a step in a cycle and we got nothing to be feared of. If I choose the afterlife concept I might know it as a certain truth that if I go to heaven or hell there will be no coming back. But who cares what I think!

I also think the thought of mortality generally switches our brain into survival mode. We are not comfortable with someone dying if we had good or rather nominal memories of that person which is our brain switching into "lost a part of life" mode and instant feeling of sadness and remorse comes in. While on the other hand people feel good with the death of someone who might have caused great harm to human society. For our-self, the brain mostly stays in passive mode because may be one of the primary function of intelligence is survival and so idea of death in so called intelligent brain is dealt with sadness too beside sometimes with some complex feelings. I sometimes have dwelled upon ideas that individual thoughts might be mortal too. They take birth in our brain, they grow and evolve over its lifetime. Sometimes they get ill and other times they grow rapidly and become powerful among all other thoughts until they die for real and you never get those thoughts just their memories. Well that was an interesting thought! This could be my thought equation.

No matter what we think of it, if we look it on a large time scale, mortality of humans might have no impact, much like what I shared in previous chapters. From a cosmic scale, we humans are just an observer and entitled to be mortal to cater the overall repeatable nature of everything in this universe. Every galaxy, star, planet, nature, animals, proteins, compound or even atom have to go through cycles of destruction and reconstruction into some other form (or sometimes the same). Sometimes planets collide to form new planets or its satellite while other times a star may die when it runs out of its nuclear fuel turning into supernova, white dwarf or may be black holes. Destructions even at those scales may also not have any impact if we see from a far-away super clusters of galaxy. At the quantum level the fundamental particles pop in and out of existence casually having half-life so small it is hard to even detect the presence of it but it doesn't affect us humans who are basically made out of those quantum particles. From a big scale mortality is just part of process and at a very small scale mortality seems almost insignificant to us, I mean our cells die every day but we are still alive. But at the right zone of scales it seems like a frightening truth to almost every human as it has impact on us if we observe it at the right scale like genocides or mass extinctions.

There are many different perspectives of seeing mortality in my mind. From getting afraid of losing everything we thought we gained in life to the most interesting perspective questioning that is mortality really means the end of anything? Some people have a very empathetic perspective while others have a realistic perspective. From a perspective of ecology, we are a part of chain so death of a living organism is important as when we die, all the protein in our bodies degrade to simpler form and turns back to earth for the plants, animals and microscopic organisms to feed on and that seems fair considering we usually consume the same from them throughout our lives. I always felt a fight inside me questioning the socially acceptable perspective of it but it seems much more complex to understand.

My thoughts about mortality may be morally wrong (or may be most of my thoughts) because I don't feel appropriately as per the society but I could be right to myself because my perspective are not there to harm any living being. I feel how I feel and not like someone the society expects me to be or what I think the society expects me to be. I think mortality sometimes enhances morals among people and they feel more human like because the idea of mortality does not explains what happens to our thoughts and memories we thought and we stored in this whole lifetime and our brain is not able to accept the end of its functioning. It is against the primary function or the corner stone of brain to have open thoughts about self-death and so may be strongly considered as a bad thought. While other times I think mortality gives meaning to the thought that the end of thoughts is just as random as anything or destined to happen and in a good sense. The death of a human is the death of thoughts, death of ones efforts and other body functions after which our bodies may well be non-functional and so may be death or the idea of being mortals is generally considered as a bad sign in human society for our own reasons.

Maybe there's a whole different story to it or maybe I am wrong!

Foot Note

 I am not a perfect human nor do I have too much knowledge of anything. I wrote this book to put my thoughts into words but I am not good with vocabularies either so there may be a lot of mistakes in these texts from grammatical to factual. I could have took more time to elaborate about many things but I am lazy so I leave most of the things to your imagination.

I don't have any intention to hurt anyone's sentiments as I understand that poor choice of words or miscommunication in language can alter the human brain chemistry making us feel happy, sad, content, outraged, offended and disappointed among others and so I would like to deeply apologize if something I wrote did that to you.

I hope you enjoyed reading.

www.ingramcontent.com/pod-product-compliance
Lightning Source LLC
Chambersburg PA
CBHW040740120726
48007CB00008B/148